About the Author

The author is married and has two grownup children. She has a passion for reading and walking in the countryside of Ireland where she lives.

Poetry

Hellen Grall

Poetry

Olympia Publishers
London

www.olympiapublishers.com
OLYMPIA PAPERBACK EDITION

Copyright © Hellen Grall 2023

The right of Hellen Grall to be identified as author of
this work has been asserted in accordance with sections 77 and 78 of
the Copyright, Designs and Patents Act 1988.

All Rights Reserved

No reproduction, copy or transmission of this publication
may be made without written permission.
No paragraph of this publication may be reproduced,
copied or transmitted save with the written permission of the publisher,
or in accordance with the provisions
of the Copyright Act 1956 (as amended).

Any person who commits any unauthorised act in relation to
this publication may be liable to criminal
prosecution and civil claims for damage.

A CIP catalogue record for this title is
available from the British Library.

ISBN: 978-1-80439-242-3

This is a work of fiction.
Names, characters, places and incidents originate from the writer's
imagination. Any resemblance to actual persons, living or dead, is
purely coincidental.

First Published in 2023

Olympia Publishers
Tallis House
2 Tallis Street
London
EC4Y 0AB

Printed in Great Britain

Dedication

I dedicate this book to my lovely family

A Country Disgraced

Come find me a story of life here today
A story that tells of our supposed forward ways
A story of love, laughter and jest
A story that will put us all to the test
A story of a country so rich in tradition
A story who sent people on missions
A story where its people fought for its right and for its freedom
A story that shows of a country that lost its own vision
A story that shows that country not in good light
A story that shows the refusal of rights
To treat like slaves mere women and children
In the land of their birth by knaves in the night
The faith that ruled was oh so strong
Has now been wiped out and completely is gone
Those that ruled with an iron fist
Are quickly realising that they are been ditched
So come tell me the story of life here today
Of a country that's changed in every way
The changes are not always good
And those in power should be more aware
That they are only in power by just a hair
They should respect the country they got
And not let the country go to pot.

A Father's Reply

It's been so long since we have talked
I was there when you were born, small and tiny
My beloved daughter who so often I nearly lost
And yet through it all, you survived and thrived
Turning into a beautiful young woman
And yet you were caused so much pain and hurt
None I could prevent.

How I wish I was there to save and protect you
The pain must have been unbearable
Do you feel so much anger towards me for leaving?
My beautiful baby girl
You have my mother's name; I wanted that for you
You were mine and mine you will remain
I have seen my grandchildren, I am so proud
You reared them well
I could not stay with you although you prayed that I would,
My pain and loss were to many to bear, I had run my race
I wanted to meet Tommie, he was waiting on me
The hurt you feel makes me so sad, for I loved you so much
I wanted to stay but had no choice
I am very proud of you
Know that that pipe smoke you smell is me; I am near, ask
me for my help
I loved you then as I love you now
Much love, Dad.

A Letter to My Mother

Dear Mam, I hope you are well and have found peace,
happiness and are untied with Dad, all your lost family
Mam, although you did try, at 15 I was left to cry alone,
standing at the grave
Nothing in common, not even friends
Drifting apart like two book ends
The pain I felt when I lost Dad
Was something that left me so very sad!
I was told, by those in the know
That I wasn't allowed my emotions to show
Not to upset you, as you grieved twice,
So I ended up paying the price
Of no relationship until near your end
I always thought your mother was supposed to be your friend
But you lost that right, to know me then
Again when you found someone else
We drifted apart, like strangers in the night
Until nearer your end, you saw the light
With outsiders, you were a wonderful friend
With your own daughter not till near the end
You gave me your wedding ring for my wedding day
Was this your way of asking me to pray?
Your life was hard, of that I know
But all I wanted was your love to show

Nearing your passing, you tried your best
To try to make up for all the rest
But I had my own family to rear
And I made a promise to myself, no love would I spare
It took a while for my daughter and me
But the fault was mine because of reason why
Talk and fight we did and do, but our make-up was good.

Angels

Have you ever seen an angel or felt its presence near
And what they are doing so very close and here
Have you ever wondered how things happen
So magical and right
Have you ever thought your angel near?
Guarding you with so much light
Have you ever found a feather so fluffy and so small?
And wondered where it came from or how it got there at all
The feathers are their special sign to let you know they are there
And if you need them at any time, then just say a prayer
It doesn't have to be very long or even one word will be enough
But if you need your special friend, he will be right there beside you
Even when times are tough
Angels are special beings, secretarial and bright
All they want for anyone is to get God's great light
To help and guide, to be at your side
Whenever there is need
They wish to help you to explore
That special door of life.

Birds

They wake us in the morning
With their beautiful dawn chorus
They cheer us until the close of day
To remind us of our sleep
But where do they go and what do they do?
In the spring, summer and autumn, we have such a chime
But in winter, they don't seem to have the time
To sing and dance and delight us all
In the winter, they are too busy gathering the fall
They nest and build and rear their young
To fly away to distance shores
We watch and gaze into the sky as these beauties swoop and fly
Birds come in colours and breeds
To brighten up our lives and dreams
Their songs enrich us with love and joy
No matter how they feel inside
There is a lesson us humans can learn;
Is to stop complaining
And enjoy the ride.

Comment on Society

At last, poor York, we knew him well
But did we, or did he smell?
Had he home or a place to rest?
Or was it a back door for his nest?
Had he a family to care for him?
Was he alone in the dark and dim?
Had he food or none at all?
Did he beg outside our hall?

Was society there with their helping hands?
Or did they walk by him with the beating of bands?
To them, he was a spot on the wall
To ignore as if not at all
Society is great, to shout and complain
But where is the help when it's needed again?

We are all guilty of passing by
And then we wonder and ask why
We refuse to help when need is most
We leave other to carry our post.

We give the bucks, and think our duty ends there
But we pass the bucks without a care
Society is great, of that there is no doubt
But maybe they should start opening their mouths.

Cup of Tea

It's the universal conversation
As you enter every door
A cup of tea you must have
And maybe some more
It's the warming of the body
On a cold and chilly day
It's the serenity of life's comfort
A way of resting on life's toll
A cup of tea helps the chat
To cure all ills, to help the cat
To clear the air
To remove the pain
To offer comfort and help the fear
To remove the tread to be an ear
We make the cuppa with skill and care
We understand the reason where
Love and life, peace and joy
Sadness and heartache
They are all there
The cup of tea offers solace and hope
To those who need it the most.

Done

To those we are
We were once before
To those who come
And wanted more
To those who see
And fail to fall
What was once now
Is gone for thou
To those who want
And never receive
Yet they still want
And try hard to believe
And yet they wonder
Of what has to come
To those who see
All has been done.

Family

Family are a complicated thing
Of that I can attest
There is no rhyme or reason
If you want to give your best
Family comes in all shapes and sizes
In all colours and creeds
Religion and gender
Family is difficult and queer
There is hurt, pain, love, hate
But family can also love where outsiders cannot see
Family have their problems
Which are often left unsaid
Feasting like a running sore unhealed
We should do more and help, but why?
Yes, family is a complicated place
Unseen and apart
Only family can heal a broken heart
At a wake or a wedding
Where drink has its toll
Promises made to be broken
How can it be good for the soul?
Family are complicated
Of that I have no doubt
But family must realise
That hate must be left out

Family must support
The occupants of its tribe
Through every fall and rise
Always at their side
Then perhaps this sadness of family being apart
What joy this world would have in it
If family had an open heart!

Free

Who am I?
I am a human being
Born on this earth
Not to destroy
But to maintain
Not to hate
But to share
Not to discourage
But to encourage
Not to break down
But to build bridges
I am me
A person who can choose
To live or not
To choose hope over fear
To choose freedom over prison
I have the right to be me
To express, to be independent
To live my life my way
I am who I am. I am me.

Heartache

It comes when you least expect it
Like a bullet from a gun
It leaves its mark forever
That never be repaired
They tell us time is a healer
But it never heals the ache
It merely moves to future
And reduces the pain
The heartache remains, of that I am quite sure
Something small and tiny will always remind you
Of those you have lost
No one cares or understands until it reaches their door They walk away untouched.

Home

The place where I live Is quite and so quaint
Not a shop in sight
Only trees and lakes
The cattle are calling their young to feed
The birds are singing louder than we need
Yet not a human in sight
The road is so busy
People rushing around
From daybreak to night, without even a break
No sound of children playing
Just stillness all around
Life has changed so much
My home has changed
No life around
The fun and laughter has disappeared
No one has time for a chat or to say hello
Too busy making dough
This place I call home though rural in sight
Has joined the rat race with all its might.

In Between

When lights go out and I am all alone
With just my thoughts for company racing
My fears are boundless without boundaries
And I wonder
Is the night
Or shall I go on?
The choice of life or a dream
No one to help, to talk or listen
God: you wonder is there one?
If you believe in one, there is one
The stage expires
You do not know
But you know one thing
You better keep up the show
A choice to make good or bad Would

Journey

As I sit here beside this beautiful water
As it glimmers in the light
The leaves are slowly turning
From their lofty height
The sky shows off its brightness
With its funny shapes of clouds
Nature in all its finery, proclaiming very loud
The beauty of its surrounding, our eyes are open wide.

The river drifts slowly along its winding way,
To bring life and beauty each and every day,
To give nourishment and love to every living thing
As it slowly travels on its way down towards the east.

The river will join the others, to form a larger base
To travel with its members at a much quicker pace,
We never know about its life, or what it has to overcome
To form from all the others, into one large one.

To us, it's just a wee river
Providing nourishment and peace
Moving slowly at a pace,
And never at a race.

Lessons of Life

The life that was will never be
Gone forever like the bees
Never to return to its joyous state
Rejected, forgotten, lost
Gone forever like a broken plate
You are miles away from
Never to depend upon, just let it be
Never helped or aided fold
Never believed what you were told
The life that was, has fallen apart
It has left behind a broken heart
One which can never be mended
No matter how you try, so end it
We must decide what to do
But that, my love, is up to you
Whether we can find another way
Whether we choose to go or stay
All that is up to you, I cannot choose
All I ask is to be true to you
And maybe you answer too.

Light

The light above shines brightly
To all of us down here
It brings its heat and healing
To everyone who is near
It helps the birds
Sing oh so fine
It brightens nature's finery to be oh so define
It makes us all happy
To see the light above
Its refreshes us
And gives us
A certain kind of love
A love that's rich and gentle
As we look out from our home
Its nature's way of telling us
Of our perfect space.

Lonely

At last poor yoked, we knew you well
But did we really?
Did he smell?
Had he a home, or a place to go
Or was it just a back door
To use for his bed?
Had he a family to care for him?
Or was he alone in the dark and dim?
Had he food or none at all?
Did he have to beg and steal outside a hall?

Was society there with their helping hands?
Or did they walk by him as a spot on the land
Society is great
To shout and complain
But where is the help
When it's needed again?
We are all guilty of passing by
And then we pose the question why
We refuse to help, when need is most
We leave it to others, to carry our post
We give the cash, and we pass it too
We have done our duty
And there is the end of it.

Society is great, of that I am sure
To complain and mane
About all the poor
But they forget, by some quirk of fate
That they could be joining the wait.

Love

Love is feeling so rare and so good
Love is a reason for people to rare
Love is an action that should cease every war
Love is a guide that helps every life
Love is what happens between a man and his wife
Love is a season that comes and that goes
Love is something that causes such woes
Love is partaking in life's finery
Love is for everyone, even for me
Love is a treat to be handled with care
Love is so special that we must all share
Love is such that must not be handled so lightly
Love is something that gives us such brightly
Love is a hope that we all hold so dear
Love asks especially to keep those close who are dear
Love is a feeling we have in our heart
Love asks us all that we never depart
Love is life that we wish for ourselves
But love can also land us in hell
Love can be forgiving and kind
Love can also play tricks on our mind
Love has a habit of coming in slowly
Even to those who don't want to know you
Love is ingrained in all that we do
Love can be beautiful, wonderful and new

Love can be patient, good and refined
Love can turn just like a dime
Love can be complicated, unknown and upset
There are times that we feel there is love we will never get
Love has many faces and shapes
Love can be wonderful given the space.

Mankind

We all hold hopes
We all share dreams,
Lights in our mind
Supposedly never to be quenched
But stopped by unbelief
A silent figure in the darkness
Spurned by regret
Mirrored by sadness
Discouraged by those who say it cannot
Destroyed by hate
All our hopes and dreams shattered
Never to be found, gone forever
Careless remarks and hurtful insults
Hope disappeared
Lights in our mind go out
They are gone, torn from us
Taken away by life's toil
The candlelight is gone
Replaced by darkness and fear.

Many Pathways of Life

There are many pathways
On our life journey
Some good, some bad
But all decisions are in our hands
The path can be varied and mixed
Straight, narrow, crooked, long or short
Adventure potholes
Whatever it may be.

We must be in control
Never waver, never stray, and never fail
Believe in oneself, true to oneself
For failure is not an option
As so many tell us
But we can fail
For failure proves we are trying
And we can rise again
Failure is part of our life's pathway
The pathway of growing in you and me
But we must not stop trying to achieve who we want to be
The way of life has many parts
Some good and some bad
There is no right or wrong to live that path
But we must choose for ourselves.

Me

I know who I am
A human being
A life
I am me
I am who I want to be
I am an individual with a
Right to live
As I see fit
With all my facilities
Entitled to fresh air, food and water
Entitled to be good, bad, whatever
With freedom to express my views, I am me
Be it right or wrong
Me to run, laugh, run, and play
Me to have my way
My skin colour doesn't matter
Black, white, yellow or red
I can be anywhere I want
I want to shout
I want everyone to see I am me
Alive and well
Nothing but fresh
I want to shout it from the clouds
I am free and bright
I am me

Like a light
I may be small in size
Not as big as some
But I believe in me
Me is who and what I am
But whatever this may be
I am but me.

My Dad

My dad was the person who I wanted to see
To see how I had lived my life to be
To be happy and watch his grandchildren be born and grow
To teach them things that he did know
To offer them kindness, compassion, hope, and love
To be the one above all others
To support me, help with words of encouragement and laughter
To keep me safe, apart from danger and all things darker
To show his grandchildren what it takes to be a human.

Not power, hurt, fight, or pain
But a friend who helped all in need
A man with secrets too painful to share
A man who appreciates the value of care
Small in stature, big in heart
My dad, how I wish we were never apart
But part we did, so you may join your son
Taken before you got to say goodbye
The pain you suffered too much to bear
One loss too many, of what you had witness in life
Taken away from your family, you went,
Dad, although I was 15, I have so many memories left.

The happy and the sad times which I had left

But now as I think, I realise how much I missed
I still often feel that I can feel your touch or smell your pipe
Is this real or just memories which feel so real
I hope I have turned out as you wanted me to be
I hope that you are happy among your loved ones
Singing, dancing and enjoying your life
Wherever you are, spare a thought for me
I miss you a lot
Thinking of you
With every tick of a clock.

My Forgotten

When I set myself down and ponder, and think of what might have been
I wonder about the babies I lost, or what they would have been
I wonder of the colour of hair, and eyes as bright as stars
I wonder where they are, or are they on a planet like Mars?
I wonder about the life they would have had, be it good or bad
I wonder, did they look like me or a mixture of us both?
I wonder would I have today the family I have
Or was it fate that intervened, and decided on what I would have?
I wonder what may have been at birthdays and at Christmas
I wonder what awaits me as I reach my final years
I wonder will they be there to greet me as I enter through that door?
Will they hug and kiss me and call me their special mum?
Will they understand and be all beautiful in that special lovely ore?
These were the ones who were never to be, yet rarely or ever forgotten by me
A mother's heath ace always remembers those who she has lost.

This Gentle Place

We travel here healing of body, soul and mind
We travel here in hope and prayer in the hope of finding thine
We come in faith and belief, wanting a miracle from our sentence
We want to stay with our loved ones but may not receive the answer.

Sad and painful this may be, we want to find a way,
To spend more, to say goodbye, we want you to have a say
Time passes so quick, we cannot leave, we are not finished
But time has passed and we must return to face our own mortality.

We arrive angry, annoyed, upset, unwilling to accept
The problems which we have; afraid and fearful,
But like magic, a light comes on
We find peace, calm, accepting and ready if we must to say goodbye.

I came to this gentle place to find a special face
A face that called and encouraged me to share
A place to help me find a reason why
And allowed me to find peace and joy.

To leave all that I hold so dear and mean so much to me
But I knew this had to be
So return I did to my place I called home
Secure in the knowledge that I am not alone.

Whatever may come, whatever may be
I am ready and waiting for me to say
Goodbye, God bless you. I am safe
On my way to my gentle place.

Our Prayers

As a child, you are taught to pray
And you do each and every day
You are told to pray to the man above
He will answer all of them
But are they sure it's a man?
Could it not be a woman?
If you when young did ask where did he live?
You were directed up to the sky above
You were told to do no wrong
As God can see way up high
But sure, you wonder as you were 5
Everything was a mortal sin
Be it wine, women and even men
As I grew and realised
That most of this was a pack of lies
God's not this as describe to a child
God is love and pity and full of smiles
But human beings have raised their store
And don't believe in prayer no more
The common trend is that this is wrong
This has become a common song
God did not create this wonderful world
It appeared all by itself
Instead of preaching about prayer
Why don't we ask what and where?

Why do the nations return to prayer?
When life is threatened and nowhere oh where
It gives us hope when all else fails
It offers us better days
Prayer is simple and can be kind
It can be done without a fuss
Its can be quite and not a must
It helps our bodies to calm our mind
Prayer can never be left behind
Prayer is simple and so pure
Prayer is something we all can do.

Pain

The pain I have is real and true
And refuses to go
Like a running tap that cannot be turned off
Those who cause the pain just walk away
As if to say, not my fault
They think they are better than you
And refuse to see what they have cost
Real pain is lost on those who cannot reply
Because of pain that caused such hurt
By those who believe they have a right
To what things they believe and camouflage
They do deny the pain they caused; 'oh, not me', they say
We have the right to be judge and jury
You lost that right, we are in charge; defend yourself
No defence appears, instead sides with enemy
Makes the pain ten thousand times worse, you are blamed
Pain with help does ease away
When assisted in a special way
It slowly fades, you cannot return to sender
Then you learn to live without fear or favour
Then you become the winner.

Passing

We pass through this life of ours just once
In a glance, we face many trials
We look into a glass
And see humans at their heights and lows
We sit and wonder why
We have but one life to live
We are passengers passing through
Passing from life to death
Passing from mortal to clay
Does our passing have an effect
On those we love and care?
Do they care or remember
Our passing or how it happened?
Do they feel sadness, loss or pain?
They come with flowers and reeds
Is it to celebrate to remember or a duty?
Has my passing done any good?
Or is it just I am gone? Good riddance!
Passing comes to all
No matter how big or small
We cannot stop it
We must accept our passing.

People-Watching

Have you ever sat and watched as people passed you by
Them rushing and the fussing and you have to wonder why
In every street and lane, on every road and plain
In all the walks of life, no matter if it rains
Have you ever wondered what keeps them going
Or where they are going to?
Have you ever wondered that that might be you too?
Have you ever wondered about their lives?
Their joy, sadness, pain, suffering, worries, hopes and dreams
Have you ever wondered about the silence as they passed?
How quickly they passed with their phone in hand
Have you ever wondered about people's shape?
Large, small, black, white; all creeds of people
Have you ever wondered about their freedom?
Or what they endure
From violence to hurt to pain to suffering
Have you ever watched and wondered why
Some are so uncared for?
That society has forgotten where we all came from
Have you ever watched these fancy cars as people step out?
And you watch and wonder what is this all about
Have you ever wondered why you are here
Or have you a purpose in life?
Have you ever wondered why people live this life?

Reason

They tell us there is a reason
For things we do not understand
But neither rhyme nor reason
Can replace the likes of you.

Your passing has quickly left
A gap that no one can fill
Your laugh, your smile, those eyes
All gone
Lying motionless, so still
While we ask many questions
While we ponder what could have been
Yet we ask and search for reasons
With no answers to be found
We did not see you come and go
We did not see you grow
We are left alone to ponder reasons
As we are left just wondering why
We take your body to the church
To see if solace we can find
But every step which we take
Brings you closer to our mind
As the funeral prayers are said
And your coffin lies in silence
We sit and think of you

Holding onto your presence
As the prayers are finally finished
And we bring your coffin out
We take you to your final resting place
Holding onto your face
As you are slowly lowered down
To the cold, dark hole in the ground
You have been taken from us for good
And the reasons we never understood
Could you not have trusted us?
To tell us what was so wrong
We could have helped you mend it
To be with us today
But you chose another route
One of which we will never know
You took your secrets with you
And left us reasoning so
God grant you peace and love
May you have found the solace that you wanted?
But you will be remembered here on earth
For the good deeds that you have done
There is no reason why you left us
Only you can answer why
All we can but hope for
Is that you are happy with God on high.

Remember

We remember the day that we were told you were coming
We remember the day we were told you were gone
We remember the day we were supposed to hold you
The joy turned to sadness as you were no more
The comments received: oh you're young, you will have another
Did they not understand what it felt for a mother?
No baby to hold, to watch and to grow
To cuddle and love, to show your new born with all your pride
All that was left was an empty space with nowhere to hide
The heartache so deep, you can't help but weep
No chance to even say goodbye
Just a space left behind and a memory to keep
Of a precious person gone to sleep.

The Chapel

The little church of clay and stone which stand upon the hill alone
Its high-rise towers and coloured windows all glazing in the sun
Its gentle size and openness in use of every day
The inside is so simple, the outside clothed in clay
All the little seat and alleys are neatly in a line
And the altar on its lofty step, it's looking so refine
The church that holds its flock in prayer and holds each and every hand
The priest upon the altar in all his robes so grand
The choir with its singing all through the little church
The holy water and prayer books waiting on every little stance
The carpet clean, all crisp and new, awaiting a brand-new bride
The church is of fine design, there is nothing to hide
When the bell does chime for the event, the congregation waits
For all those who are outside, waiting at the gate
The bell does call each and every one to come join them at the altar
Where people come to reflect and pray and even may have faltered
The little church does stand within a graveyard old as it can be
This little church is standing guard on everything you see

It carries those to their final home under the fine old trees
To carry souls to their reward, in life and final thee
The little church is part of life though standing on its own
No house or any humans, no, nothing to atone
It's part of this community, of that I can attest
I will be there, someday, in time for my finality of rest.

The Human Race

The human race are a funny old creed
Watching all with all their needs
Racing and running
Each and everywhere
Going about
Here and there
We are the human beings
Supposed to mind the earth
Yet we destroy rather than maintain
No heart to stand for good
We are all unique, with individual needs
We are all so different
Colours, race and creeds
We share this planet
With all its life forms
We cannot be allowed to deform
We are all responsible for each living thing
We are supposed to be
The superior being
We are made up of different genders
Each entitled to love and support
No matter who or what we are
The colour of our skin
Shouldn't decide who we are
We must stand together

To face every war
To face those who hate and divide
Whether by paper or those that hide
We must stand shoulder to shoulder.

Against All Who Come

We must understand the meaning of love
Hunan beings, we are a funny old lot
Some good, some bad, some not so hot
We all share this world
In good times and bad
We must be true to one another
And move forward in peace.

The Land

The sky above, the land below
Why is everything going so slow?
The birds that sing, the animals rare
A question to be asked is what and where?
They rear their young in peace and quiet
As you are quietly sitting there
Watching, waiting for the young to appear
Suddenly, they all are here
Running and jumping and flying high
Loving the weather from the sky
The weather is warm, the pickings are sweet
They creatures of life all have their meet
They come and the go, including the bees
Making beautiful honey and wonderful mead
We listen and we watch
We laugh and enjoy
What a wonderful bounty this land can provide
For humans and creatures and glory to be
What a wonderful miracle
This land can see
To use to love it and care for true
Food aplenty too for that can thee
The land is precious and so grand
We must it hand in hand
With those who we share this gift
We must be gentle with the land.

The Old Man

As I sat upon the harbour and watched out to the sea
I saw an old man walking, his hands against his knee
He rubbed his knees so gently as though he was in pain
And yet he kept on walking, just looking at the train
He wore a cap and trousers of the times of the sea
He was once a fine young sailor, but now he could not be
He looked out to the ocean and all the boats he sailed
The life he had when he was young on those beautiful, fine waves
But now he could no longer take a ship to sea
All he could do was watch and stare and say that was once me
The old man walked along in a quite calmly way
Talking with him and speaking of the day
The people passed him with no kind word or greeting fine
Just pushed their way away from him as he was a dime
The old man sat down on an old wooden bench, and gazed out to sea
To remember from the distance his travels and the people whom he had meet
The old man did get up as the evening began to close
To head off home, the lonely road not a sinner to know
No one knows where he lives or if he lives alone
Each day he comes and sits alone on this beautiful strand
He sits and dreams of days gone by of when he was a boy
And hopes the good lord will take him so that he can find some joy.

The Seasons

The seasons do come and go as in the case of life
Spring, summer, autumn then winter comes as the nights go dark
Spring and summer bring days of sunshine and of light
Autumn days bring loads of colour and a shortening of the bright
Winter days bring cold and rain and many days of snow
And each thing covers its head to find somewhere to go
The seasons are in a block of four
But each with its array
To live a life, to hope and sing
At the end of each new day
To watch the birds upon the sky
To follow all the way
To wear with age like a fine wine
To march our lives like a fine old wine
To watch the fruits and harvest come
Upon the trees so high
To enjoy and dance in the midnight air
To be one again like thine
To walk and gather the seasons' riches
To dine on all a new
To farm together the wood and turf
As in the days of old
To watch and wait as the seasons come as we slowly do grow old.

Time

The time that was
Can sometimes be
Yesterday, today, tomorrow, *qui*
Count time by clock, we often to
But every second brings life anew.

Time cannot be counted
Be it day or night
That is why
Time is always right.

The time that is 'cannot' never return
Lost and gone forever,
Only found in our memories
Wishing it back.

Time changes all lives, above and beneath
From birth till death, time takes its toll
It has no respect of age or wealth
Enclosing all of us in its fold

Time marches on, all through life
With no thought for those who lose and fall It has no respect for health or life
What would life be like without time? I for one would like to know.

Users

Life gives many options
To walk upon this earth
To be provided with all our needs
Yet people seem to forget
They think they are the masters
Of earth's bounties and fruits
But they waste so much unseemly
And loses all our treasures
We must live in harmony Be mindful of what we have
We must respect what is left And care for it with depth
There is no endless supply of bounties It will come to an end
We must care for our precious cargo And care as we go.

Village Life

The village is quite
Not a person in sight
No sound or noise
Not even a light
The place seems so empty of happiness and peace
In its centre, stands the church
Where people gathered to pray and worshiped
Its setting is beautiful
So eerie and still
Surrounded by nature
On top of the hills
Its ancient and legends told far and wide
But the village is quite
As it stands by its side
The people are few
The school seems so small
Hardly a noise
Yet it all seems to fit
This small rural place
Like a ball in your hand
The village will stir
Was once so full of life
But no more
The village has come to its end.

Words

Words are used in everyday
For thoughts, hopes, feelings, dreams
Angry words, peaceful words
Strange words, sorrowful words
Written down and often spoken
Often broken, unrecognisable words
Often used as seldom thoughts
Words of love and loss
Words of fun and of laughter
Words of silence, words of pain
Words misused to hurt
Words used in haste
Words of kindness and of gentleness
Music poetry in all life
Special words
Words used in every way maker of life
Housed in our heart
Never in waste
Words give hope when all else fails
Words are nought.

You

It could be me
And I be you
Your life would change dramatically
You see the hurt and the pain
Which has been put on me in vain
As a train goes on its tracks
I shouldn't have had to deal with all that
I should be out and about
Instead, I am left all alone
To ponder, think and atone
For what or whom
You may ask?
To my own self
For being bullied and ashamed
So, you see
If you were me and I were you
You would understand the hurt too
Be aware of what has happened
Because you were part of it too
But not to be
So it remains
You be you
And me be me.